F is for Fenway

America's Oldest Major League Ballpark

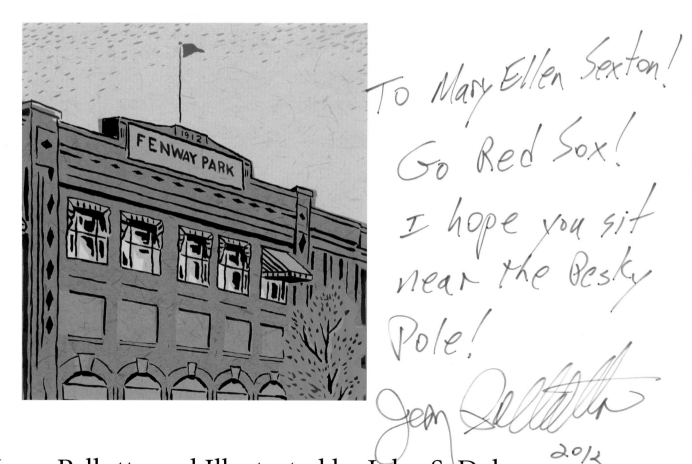

To Mary Ellen Sexton!
Go Red Sox!
I hope you sit
near the Pesky
Pole!

Jerry Pallotta
2012

Written by Jerry Pallotta and Illustrated by John S. Dykes

Sleeping Bear Press wishes to thank and acknowledge Helen L. Wilbur
for her valuable contribution to this book.

Text Copyright © 2012 Jerry Pallotta
Illustration Copyright © 2012 John S. Dykes

Sleeping Bear Press™

315 East Eisenhower Parkway, Suite 200
Ann Arbor, MI 48108
www.sleepingbearpress.com

© 2012 Sleeping Bear Press is an imprint of Gale, a part of Cengage Learning.

Printed and bound in the United States

10 9 8 7 6 5 4 3 2 1

Library of Congress Cataloging-in-Publication Data

Pallotta, Jerry.
F is for fenway : America's oldest major league ballpark / written
by Jerry Pallotta ; Illustrated by John Dykes.
p. cm.
Summary: "Historic and nostalgic Fenway Park is introduced from A to Z
with rhyming poems and informational text. Topics include green monster,
Jimmy Fund, Kenmore Square, Peskys Pole, the lone red seat, and Van Ness
Street."-- Provided by publisher.
ISBN 978-1-58536-788-7 (hardback)
1. Fenway Park (Boston, Mass.)--History--Juvenile literature.
2. Boston Red Sox (Baseball team)--History--Juvenile literature.
3. Alphabet--Juvenile literature. I. Dykes, John, ill. II. Title.
GV416.B674P35 2012
796.357'640974461--dc23
2011042563

Boston's Fenway Park has been called America's most beloved ballpark because so many people believe it is loved more than any other ballpark. The building of Fenway Park began in 1911, and the park was finished in 1912. It is the oldest major league ballpark still in use today. The first major league baseball game played in Fenway was on April 20th, 1912, between the Boston Red Sox and the New York Highlanders—the team that would later become the New York Yankees. As an estimated 27,000 fans watched from their seats, the Red Sox beat the Highlanders 7–6 in 11 innings of baseball. The Red Sox would go on to win the 1912 World Series against the New York Giants in Fenway Park.

Boston's mayor in 1912, John Fitzgerald, threw out the ceremonial first pitch before the start of the first game. His grandson, John Fitzgerald Kennedy, who was born in 1917, would become the 35th president of the United States.

A is also for American League. Fenway is an American League ballpark. Major League Baseball has a National League and an American League.

A is for America's Most Beloved Ballpark

For baseball lovers everywhere
the experience they want to share
is Fenway's magic and mystique,
which make this classic park unique.

The bullpen is where the pitchers wait and warm up during the game before they start pitching. No one knows for certain where the name *bullpen* came from, but there are many theories. The most popular theory is that baseball's bullpens look like the pens where bulls are held at a rodeo or a bullfight.

At Fenway Park, the bullpens are in right field, next to the stands. In 1940, Red Sox officials decided to build bullpens for two reasons. The long, rectangular-shaped area gave pitchers a safe place to stay and enough room to practice their pitches. The bullpens shortened the length of a home run hit to right field by 20 feet from 400 feet to 380 feet. The shortened distance ultimately helped the Red Sox win games in Fenway Park. This is partly because Ted Williams, the team's new left-handed power hitter, sent most of his home runs to right field.

A team's relief pitching staff is sometimes called the *bullpen*.

B is for Bullpen

Fastball, change-up, slider, curve,
warm your arm, steel your nerve.
Fake 'em with your knuckleball,
ready when you get the call.

When the park first opened, most of the fans were men. At the games, the men wore suits, ties, and derbies. A derby is a stiff hat made of felt with a dome-shaped top and narrow brim. Now the crowds are more family-oriented with moms, dads, kids, aunts, and uncles attending the games.

Many people use the term *Red Sox Nation* to describe the official fan club of the Boston Red Sox. Interested fans can buy citizenship in the Red Sox Nation. Red Sox Nation members receive a commemorative citizenship card, can take advantage of official team store discounts, and head to the game early to watch batting practice. According to the *Boston Globe,* staff writer Nathan Cobb coined the term *Red Sox Nation* in 1986.

The crowd that comes to Fenway to watch baseball is sometimes referred to as the Fenway faithful. On September 22, 1937, the all-time sellout crowd for a baseball game at Fenway Park included 47,627 fans. They were there to watch a doubleheader between the Boston Red Sox and the New York Yankees. Today's fire laws now prevent that many fans from entering the park.

The 100th anniversary game in April 2012 is recorded as the 713th consecutive sellout crowd at Fenway Park—a major league record!

C is for Crowd

From all over, the loyal fans
fill the bleachers, the boxes, the stands.
Fenway roars in celebration.
That's the voice of the Red Sox Nation.

In professional baseball, the players don't sit out in the open next to the fans. The players are in the dugout along with the manager and his assistant coaches. After coming off the field, players exchange gloves for bats and helmets, and then wait in the dugout for their turn at bat. There are two dugouts, one for the home team and one for the visiting team. This design allows for an unobstructed view for the fans and protection for those in the dugout.

At Fenway Park, the home dugout is in foul territory between home plate and first base. The visiting team's dugout is on the third-base side. Each dugout is attached to a clubhouse where the players have their lockers and showers.

D d

D is for Dugout

Review the signals, plan and scheme,
watch the moves of the other team.
Analyze strategy, make revisions,
a game's won or lost on those dugout decisions.

E e

E is for Elephants

The kids of Boston saved their cents
to buy three talented elephants,
who, after a Fenway celebration,
became a Franklin Park sensation.

1912

FENWAY PARK

Surprisingly, the largest crowd ever to attend Fenway Park was not there for a baseball game, a concert, or a political event. It was the day 50,000 kids showed up to watch three elephants parade into the park. On June 6, 1914, the elephants Mollie, Waddy, and Tony were bought from a circus for $6,000 with pennies donated by kids from all over the city. Massachusetts Governor David Walsh and Boston Mayor James Michael Curley were also at Fenway Park to celebrate the successful fundraiser, called Pennies for Elephants. After a walk around the field, the elephants went to their new home in Boston's Franklin Park Zoo.

Ff

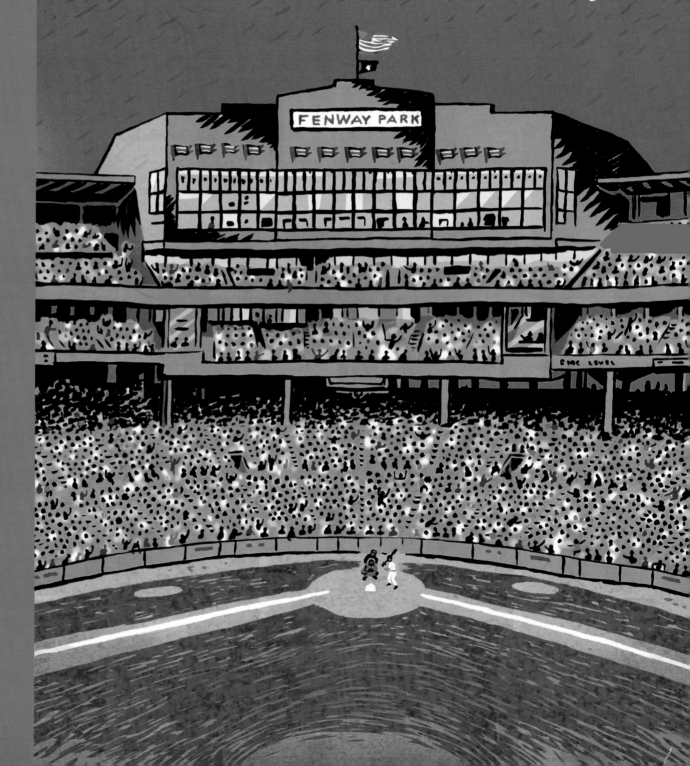

F is for Fenway Park

It isn't just a ballpark; it's Boston's sacred ground.
From the furthest bleacher seats to the pitching mound.
A shrine to the game of baseball, nothing feels as right
as watching a game at Fenway Park on a perfect summer night.

Fenway Park was built next to a marshland. It got its name from the Norwegian word *fen*, which means "swamp." It is the home of the Boston Red Sox. If someone were to ask you what Boston is most famous for, most believe it would be safe (and accurate) to reply, Fenway Park. The park is considered a sports cathedral and holds the record for the greatest number of consecutive sold-out games by a major league baseball team. All these fans don't seem to mind that Fenway also leads the league in the number of seats that have an obstructed view.

Fenway Park is now the oldest major league ballpark in use. Tiger Stadium, home of the Detroit Tigers, was built during the same era but was torn down in 2009. Comiskey Park, home of the Chicago White Sox, was built in 1910 but was demolished in 1991.

Today the park's seating capacity for night games is 37,493, while seating capacity for day games is slightly less at 37,065. During a day game some center field seats are covered with a dark-colored tarp serving as backdrop that provides batters with a better view of the pitch.

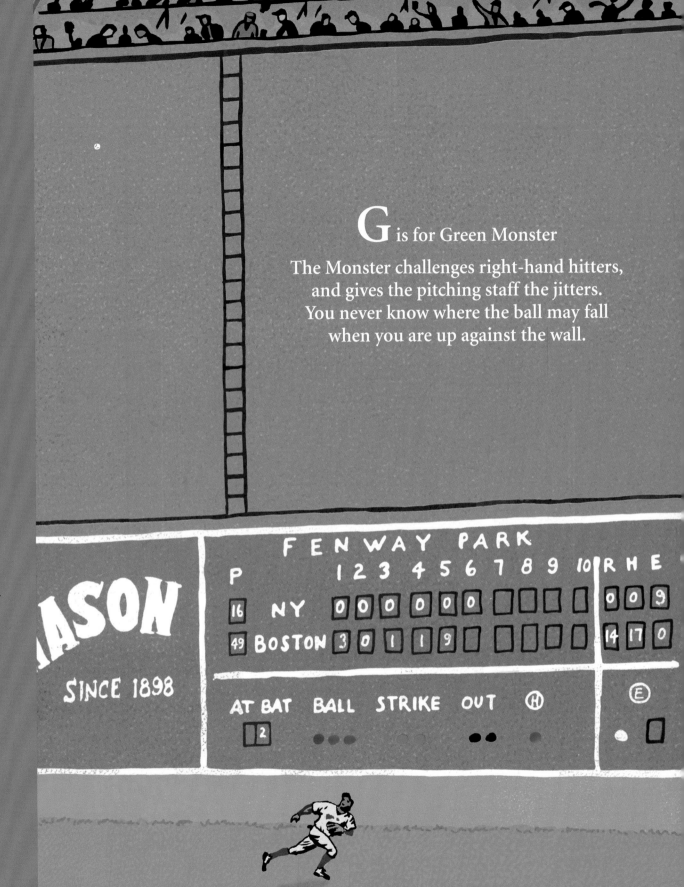

The highest wall in a major league baseball park is the left field wall at Fenway Park. It stands 37 feet tall and is 240 feet long. The original wall was 25 feet tall and made of wood. It was supported by a mound of dirt nicknamed Duffy's Cliff. Red Sox left fielder Duffy Lewis was so skilled at running up the 10-foot mound of earth to make plays that it became his namesake.

The wall was covered in sheet metal in 1934 and advertisements were painted all over it. In 1947, the Red Sox decided to repaint the wall green. Benjamin Moore is the only company that makes the special paint color called Fenway Green. It was not long before Boston fans christened this wall the Green Monster, or, if you want to sound like a Boston local, the Green Monstah!

Wally the Green Monster is the Boston Red Sox's official mascot. He is described as being pretty big, and he apparently doesn't like to say how much he weighs. Wally attends all the home games at Fenway Park.

G is for Green Monster

The Monster challenges right-hand hitters, and gives the pitching staff the jitters. You never know where the ball may fall when you are up against the wall.

Home runs can be described as in the park or out of the park. If you hear fans yell: it's a jack, a bomb, a four-bagger, a dinger, a smash, out-a-here, over the wall, a gopher shot, moon shot, a bleacher burner, a tape measure, or a round tripper, it means the batter has hit a ball out of the ballpark. Hugh Bradley, playing for the Boston Red Sox, hit the first home run at Fenway Park on April 26, 1912. The ball went over the left field wall.

Down the left field line a Fenway Park home run is 310 feet away from home plate; straightaway center field is 385 feet; the triangle is 420 feet; and into the right field bullpen is 380 feet. The longest home run ever hit at Fenway was Ted Williams's 502-foot home run. Carlton Fisk hit a walk-off home run in Game 6 of the 1976 World Series. Manny Ramirez hit a home run that may have been longer than Ted Williams's homer but we will never know because it hit a light pole. It is officially listed at 501 feet. The New York Yankees' Bucky Dent hit a famous home run into the nets during a one-game play-off at Fenway Park against the Boston Red Sox on October 2, 1978. And the Red Sox lost the game.

H h

H is for Home Run

It's out of the park; it's over the wall,
a tater, four bagger, it touches them all.
A dinger, a moon shot, it's out of this sphere,
and for one lucky fan, it's a great souvenir.

Ii

The Fenway Park infield is different from most major league infields because it is close to the stands. There is less foul-ball territory, so more pop-ups and foul balls end up in the seats, giving players much less opportunity to catch those balls. As a result, batting averages are higher at Fenway Park. A ballplayer once said, "Around the league you see colors when you look in the stands, at Fenway you see faces."

The Fenway infield is made of crushed brick. This gives it a reddish-orange color.

I is for Infield

Just when you think you've got the stop,
the ball can take a wicked hop.
The infield turf's a tricky place.
Don't look now—a man's on base.

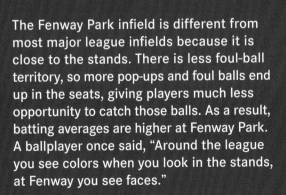

J is for the Jimmy Fund

A great team lends its hearts and hands
to champion its smallest fans.
Giving hope and inspiration
with every Jimmy Fund donation.

JIMMY FUND

JIMMY FUND WALK

J j

The Jimmy Fund is a special charity that raises money for Boston's Dana-Farber Cancer Institute. The fund started in 1948 when a national radio show organized a surprise for a young cancer patient named Jimmy, while he was in the hospital being treated. Members of his favorite baseball team, the Boston Braves, came to his room with signed baseballs, tickets, and caps. The visit was broadcast and ended with Jimmy and the players singing "Take Me Out to the Ball Game." Listeners sent in donations to fulfill the boy's request for a TV so he could watch his team play, and the funds also supported cancer research and care. When the Braves left Boston for Milwaukee in 1953, the Red Sox adopted the Jimmy Fund as its official charity. Red boxes with a money slot are located all around Fenway Park. Players and fans are very generous. The fund now raises more than $1 million each week by hosting many different fundraising events. Thousands of kids with cancer have been cured. This is another reason why Fenway Park is a special place.

K is for Kenmore Square

To Kenmore Square on the Green Line
underneath the CITGO sign,
the brick façade on Yawkey Way,
you're here to see the Red Sox play.

YAWKEY WAY

BROOKLINE

FENWAY STATION
Ⓣ
GREEN LINE

ONE WAY

CITGO

TO
KENMORE
STATION

BOSTON
BASEBALL

K k

Where is Fenway Park? Near Kenmore
Square! Starting in 1914, fans were able to
take a trolley car to the ball game. Today the
excitement starts when the conductor says,
"Next stop, Kenmore Square." On game day,
almost everyone on the crowded train gets
off, and a river of Red Sox fans flows into
the ballpark. This is what you will hear on
the walk to the park: "Anyone need tickets?"
"Hey, get your T-shirts." "Peanuts here!"
"Best sausage in Boston."

Kenmore Square is also home to the CITGO
sign. You can see the famous sign from the
park. Every now and then it looks as though
a home run could travel all the way to
Kenmore Square and hit the neon sign.

K is also the symbol used for a strikeout
in a baseball scorebook. And a backward
K (Ʞ) is a symbol for a strikeout when the
batter doesn't swing and is "caught looking"
as the strike goes across home plate.

Fenway Park is the only major league park with a ladder in the field of play. Attached to the Green Monster, the ladder was used by the grounds crew to retrieve home run balls from the netting above the wall. The radio and TV commentators used to say, "It's in the nets!" when a batted ball landed there. New seating on top of the Monster has replaced the nets. The ladder no longer has a purpose, but it remains. Batters have hit the ladder for a routine single or double. Only twice has the ball caromed off the ladder for an inside-the-park home run. If the ball gets caught in the ladder, it is a ground-rule triple. This is the only ground-rule triple in major league baseball. But in the first 100 years of Fenway Park baseball, this has never happened.

L is for Ladder

Once used to get balls from the nets,
against the wall the ladder sets.
Except for the very lucky batter
the ladder doesn't matter.

L l

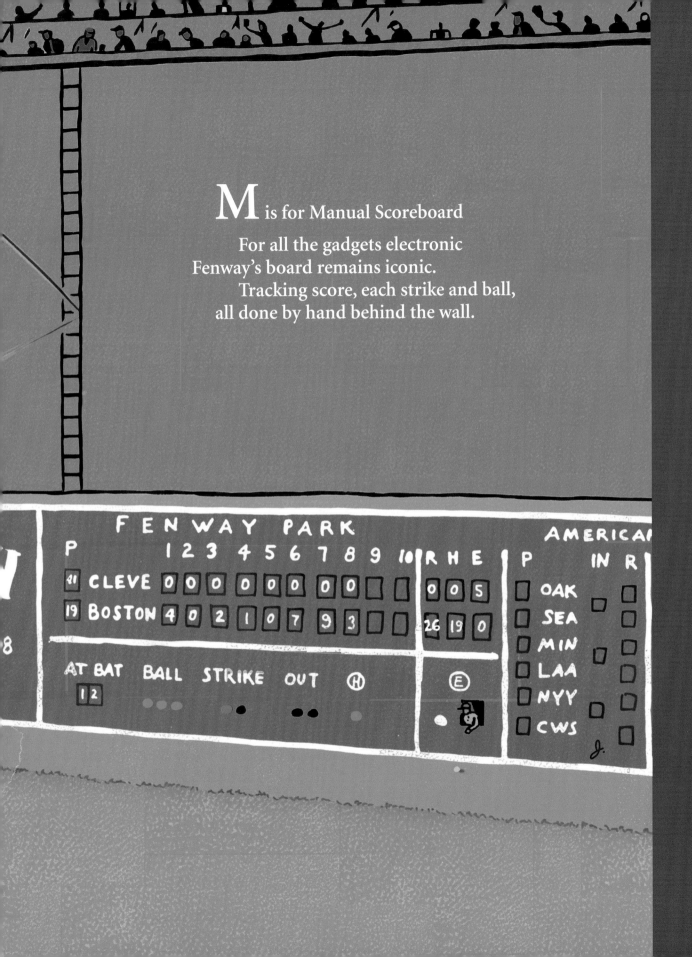

M is for Manual Scoreboard

For all the gadgets electronic
Fenway's board remains iconic.
Tracking score, each strike and ball,
all done by hand behind the wall.

Manual means something is made or operated by hand. In this case, it's the Fenway Park manual scoreboard, located at the base of the Green Monster. This scoreboard was installed in 1934. Between innings and as runs are scored, scoreboard operators inside the wall provide updates. They can watch the game through narrow slits in the scoreboard's surface. Strikes and outs are signified by red lights and balls are shown using green lights.

Signatures of former players are on the walls of the room behind the manual scoreboard. Here's a Fenway secret: the initials of former owners of the Boston Red Sox, Thomas and Jean Yawkey, appear in Morse code on the scoreboard.

M m

N is for Numbers

Elected to the Hall of Fame,
10 years a Red Sox, played the game.
For players honored and admired,
all their numbers are retired.

Up on the right field deck at Fenway Park are the numbers 1, 4, 6, 8, 9, 14, 27, and 42. They also appear outside the park behind the bleachers. These are the retired numbers of famous Red Sox players. Once a number is retired, no Red Sox player will ever wear that number again. Jackie Robinson was the first African American to play major league baseball. His number has been retired by every major league team. He played for the Brooklyn Dodgers from 1947 to 1956.

#1 Bobby Doerr played his entire 14-season career with the Red Sox.

#4 Joe Cronin was the first modern-day player to become a league president. He was also a manager, and a general manager.

#6 Johnny Pesky is known as Mr. Red Sox.

#8 Carl Yastrzemski was the first former Little League player to be elected to the National Baseball Hall of Fame.

#9 Ted Williams is known as "the greatest hitter who ever played baseball."

#14 Jim Rice played 16 years with the Red Sox.

#27 Carlton Fisk hit the walk-off 12th-inning, game-winning home run in Game 6 of the 1975 World Series.

#42 Jackie Robinson's number has been retired by every major league team.

Happy 100th Birthday to Fenway Park! The first baseball game played at Fenway Park was on April 9, 1912, when the Boston Red Sox played against Harvard University to try out its new park. The first major league baseball game was scheduled for April 12 that year, but rain postponed the game. Finally on April 20, 1912, the Boston Red Sox defeated the New York Highlanders in Fenway Park. The opening of the new park was not a big story that day. It was overshadowed by the tragic news of the sinking of the RMS *Titanic*.

Grandstand seats cost 10¢ in 1912. In 2012, they cost $50. Box seats used to cost 50¢; now they cost $125. There are some seats in the park that cost $300 per game. A private corporate roof box costs $250,000 for the whole season. A hot dog used to cost 5¢; now it costs $4. A Red Sox player used to get paid $1,000 for the whole season. Some players now get paid $15 million per year.

It has been 100 years of World Series, major meltdowns, great athletes, crazy fans, annoying curses, lots of tears, and generations of memories.

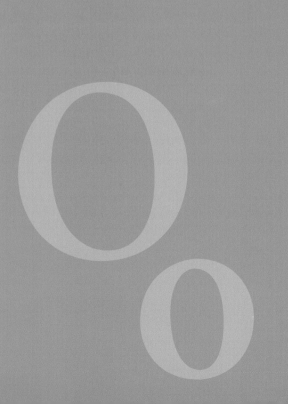

O is for One Hundred Years

Go back in time at Fenway Park; join the crowd on Yawkey Way.
Sit in the seat your grandpa sat in to watch the Red Sox play.
Remember the greats who played here, a link to baseball's past,
a century of tradition, of memories that last.

The Pesky Pole is near the foul line in right field. The bright yellow pole itself is in fair territory. A home run off the Pesky Pole is only 302 feet from home plate. It is considered a cheap home run, meaning the batter didn't have to hit the ball very far to score a home run. Usually a hit of that distance is a routine pop fly out. The pole is named after Johnny Pesky, who hit only 17 home runs during his 10-year career. He was a popular player who blooped a few home runs around the pole.

If you ever see the Pesky Pole up close, you'll see that it has been signed by thousands of fans. Johnny Pesky kissed it during the official dedication ceremony on September 26, 2006, which was his 87th birthday. Quite an honor!

P is for Pesky's Pole

Mr. Red Sox, number 6,
  got to base on bunts and hits.
For one home run that won the game
  the right foul pole bears his name.

Pp

Q is for Quarter

You can't get much for a quarter these days,
but back at the start of the baseball craze,
a dime would get you a bleacher seat
with plenty left over for something to eat.

On opening day in 1912 a grandstand bleacher seat ticket cost 10¢—only 10¢! There were also tickets being sold for 25¢—only a quarter! A family of four people could get into Fenway Park for $1.

Pretend you are a kid on opening day and your grandfather gave you a quarter to go to the ball game. You could buy a grandstand seat for 10¢ and then with your change buy two hot dogs and a drink. Imagine what you could do with two quarters.

Qq

Boston

THURSDAY, OCTOBER 28, 2004

FINALLY!!

FIRST SINCE 1918

SOX COMPLETE SWEEP

R is for Red Sox

Devoted fans love the Olde Towne Team
from Bambino's Curse to the Impossible Dream.
The hopes, disappointments, the jeers, and the cheers
brought the World Series win after 86 years.

R r

Fenway Park is the home field of the Boston Red Sox, playing in the American League Eastern Division. Before taking the name Boston Red Sox, the team was called the Boston Americans, a baseball organization that was started in 1901. The name Red Sox literally comes from the red socks that then-owner John I. Taylor chose to have his team wear in late 1907. The team decided to print *sox* instead of *socks* on their uniforms because three letters fit better than five letters. Interestingly, *sox* appears in the *American Heritage Dictionary* as a plural of *sock*.

The Curse of the Bambino is what many people call the result of Red Sox owner Harry Frazee's decision to sell Babe Ruth to the New York Yankees in December of 1919. After the sale, the Boston Red Sox would have to wait 86 years, until 2004, to celebrate a World Series win.

When the Red Sox made it to the World Series in 1967 for the first time in 21 years, the accomplishment was called the Impossible Dream. They went from last place to first place in one year. Prior to this time, the team had not had a winning season in 8 years.

TEAMMATES

S is for Statue

The Teammates stand outside Gate B,
shoulder to shoulder as pals should be.
Playing the season that never ends,
baseball legends, lifelong friends.

Behind Fenway Park on the corner of Van Ness and Ipswich Streets, there are two statues. One is of famous Red Sox teammates—Ted Williams, Bobby Doerr, Johnny Pesky, and Dom DiMaggio. These men played together for seven years and were friends for life. The group didn't win the World Series together, but they were on the team that won 104 games in 1946. Each was named to the All-Star Team and is a member of the Red Sox Hall of Fame. The plaque on the statue also points out that they served in World War II a combined 11 years. These players and *The Teammates* are an inspiration to all fans.

The other statue is of Ted Williams and a young boy. When you first see the statue, it may appear as if the boy hopes to grow up to be like Ted Williams, and someday play for the Red Sox. Another look at the statue reveals Ted is reaching out and handing his cap to the boy—a gesture meant to protect the boy. Ted's favorite charity was the Jimmy Fund. Ted is reaching out to Jimmy, the young boy with leukemia, who was the embodiment of the Jimmy Fund.

Ss

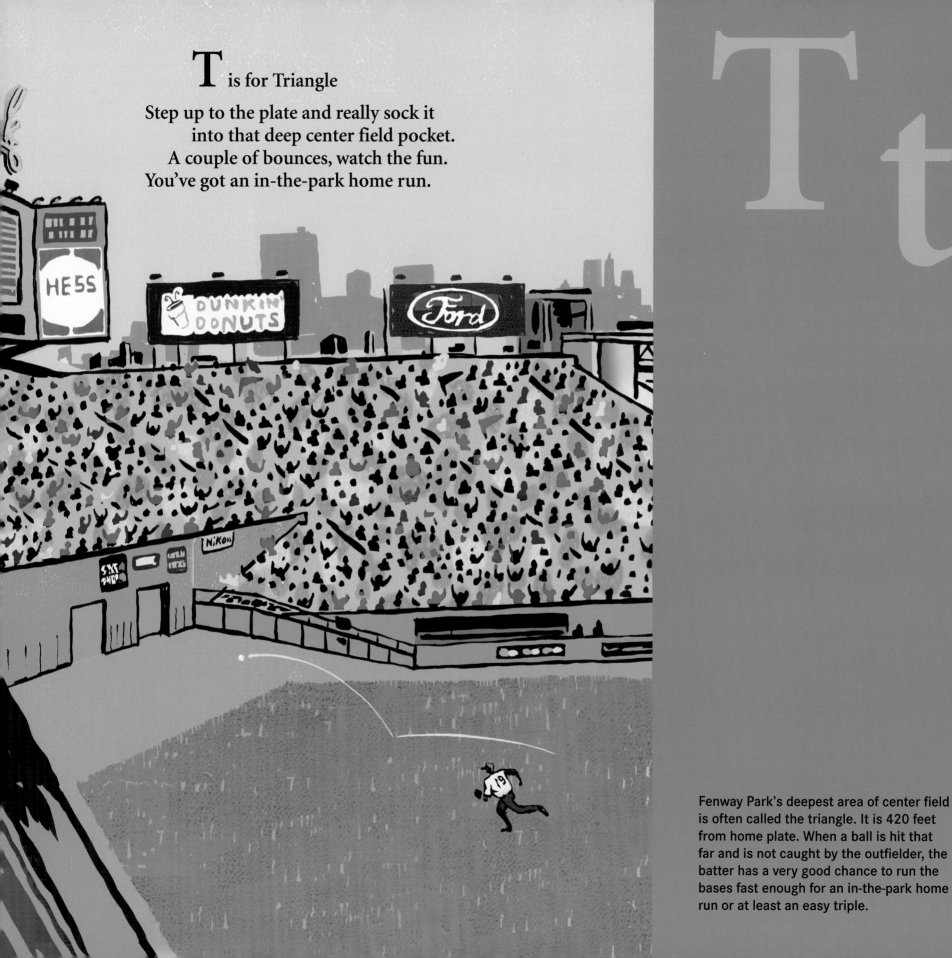

T is for Triangle

Step up to the plate and really sock it
    into that deep center field pocket.
A couple of bounces, watch the fun.
You've got an in-the-park home run.

HESS

DUNKIN' DONUTS

Ford

Nikon

Fenway Park's deepest area of center field is often called the triangle. It is 420 feet from home plate. When a ball is hit that far and is not caught by the outfielder, the batter has a very good chance to run the bases fast enough for an in-the-park home run or at least an easy triple.

T t

"Sweet Caroline," a 1969 Neil Diamond song, is sung most often during or just following the eighth inning of a Red Sox game at Fenway Park. Fans seem to know all the words. And a Red Sox win at Fenway ends with "Dirty Water" as sung by the Standells. It is another unofficial song. Here is a famous lyric: "Oh! Oh! Boston, you're my home!"

Naturally, the fans also sing "Take Me Out to the Ball Game." All fans in major league baseball sing this one. But at Fenway, some words are changed. " ... if the Red Sox don't win it's a shame!"

During the World Series in 1903, the fans sang "Tessie" from the musical *The Silver Slipper*. The song was played again in 2004, the year the Red Sox won the World Series after 86 years.

A red-tailed hawk is the unofficial mascot that lives at Fenway Park. He used to live in the light towers above the third base line. The grounds crew did all it could to scare him off. He simply moved to the light tower over by the bleachers.

U u

U is for Unofficial Anthem

Whether the home team's losing or winning,
we all sing together in the eighth inning.
Thousands of voices, a stirring rendition
of "Sweet Caroline"—a Fenway tradition.

Fenway Park is not symmetrical like most major league ballparks are. It has a strange shape because the streets around it all existed before the park was built. The five streets around the park are Brookline Avenue, Jersey Street, Lansdowne Street, Ipswich Street, and Van Ness Street. Jersey Street has been renamed Yawkey Way.

Thanks to the city of Boston, Yawkey Way becomes part of the park during ball games because it is closed to vehicle traffic. Fans can exit the park, cross Yawkey Way, and shop at the Red Sox souvenir store.

It is common for a home run to be hit over the Green Monster onto Lansdowne Street. A Red Sox radio announcer might say, "That ball was crushed and is now on Lansdowne Street!" A lucky fan outside the park may even catch it.

If you want to see your favorite player, or find out what car he is driving, then go to the players' parking lot on Van Ness Street over by Gate D.

...going...going....gone!

V is for Van Ness

Five streets near Beantown's old Back Bay
create the shape of famed Fenway.
Its size is part of the attraction—
fans are closer to the action.

Right field at Fenway Park is nicknamed Williamsburg after famous Hall of Fame player Ted Williams. Being a left-handed pull hitter he naturally hit to right field. Considered the best hitter that ever played the game, Ted is the last player to have had a batting average over .400. He hit .406 in 1941. In his career he also hit 521 home runs—an amazing feat considering he spent five years as a U.S. Marine fighter pilot serving in World War II and the Korean War.

At Fenway Park, straightaway right field is 380 feet from home plate; at Yankee Stadium, right field is only 320 feet away. Ted Williams might have hit many more home runs if Yankee Stadium had been his home field.

Ted Williams had many nicknames—Splendid Splinter, Teddy Ballgame, and The Kid—and he was often described as the greatest hitter who ever played the game. Boston sports-writers coined the name Williamsburg.

W is for Williamsburg

This part of the field honors his name:
the Splendid Splinter, Teddy Ballgame.
A home run hitter who left his mark.
One of the legends of Fenway Park.

X _marks the spot_

Bleacher seats are green
except the one that's red.
That's where the longest home run fell,
a blast from the awesome Ted.

At Fenway Park there are a lot of red seats. Most of them are in the box-seat sections of the park near the field. If you look out at the bleachers, all the seats are green except one seat, one famous red seat in Section 42, Row 37, Seat 21.

The lone red seat marks the spot where Ted Williams hit the longest recorded home run in Fenway Park. It traveled 502 feet. According to legend, it hit a sleeping New York Yankee fan in the head and woke him up. Mickey Mantle, a New York Yankee, and Ted Williams are the only two batters to have hit a ball onto the right field roof above sections 1, 2, and 3 in Fenway Park.

And let's not forget a nine-time all-star, Jimmy Foxx. His nicknames were "Double X" and "the Beast."

One of the greatest rivalries in sports is the Boston Red Sox versus the New York Yankees. They have played each other more than 2,000 times in the last 100 years. Both teams play in the American League Eastern Division. Some feel the rivalry began in 1919 when then–Boston Red Sox owner Harry Frazee sold Babe Ruth to the New York Yankees.

The Yankees' team color is blue; the Red Sox's team color is red. The Yankees wear pinstripes; the Red Sox wear solids. Yankee Stadium favors left-handed hitters; Fenway Park favors right-handed hitters. The Yankees once considered trading Joe DiMaggio, their biggest star, for Ted Williams, the Red Sox's biggest star.

Y is for Yankees Rivalry

From the opening pitch to the final out,
you can feel the excitement, there is no doubt.
The air's electric, the fans aflame—
it's a Red Sox–Yankees game.

Zz

Fenway was built for warm-weather outdoor baseball, and Zamboni™ is the brand name for a machine that cleans the surface of an ice rink. So what is a Zamboni™ doing in a baseball park book?

On January 1, 2010, the National Hockey League Winter Classic hockey game was held at Fenway Park. A temporary portable ice rink was built on the infield, and a Zamboni™ was used to resurface the ice. That day, the Boston Bruins beat the Philadelphia Flyers 2–1 in overtime. Boston area youth hockey leagues and the general public skated on the ice in Fenway Park prior to the Winter Classic game on New Year's Day.

In 1949, Frank Zamboni invented a motorized ice-resurfacing machine. Zamboni™ ice-resurfacing machines are used in hockey arenas and on ice rinks around the world.

Other events hosted in Fenway Park:
- Boxing
- Catholic Mass
- College and high school ice hockey
- College baseball
- Fund-raisers
- International soccer
- Jazz festival
- Lacrosse
- Presidential speech
- Professional and college football
- Rock concerts
- Wrestling

Z is for Zamboni™

In January's gloom and chill
sports fans get a special thrill.
Fenway's gleaming ice awaits
so bundle up and lace your skates.